MVFOL

POSTAL CARRIER

D0038798

by Sheila Rivera

first step nonfiction

Lerner Publications · Minneapolis

What does a postal carrier do?

She sorts letters.

He drives.

He says hello.

She carries the mail.

He brings me a letter.

Do you know a postal carrier?